STUDIES IN THE ROMANCE LANGUAGES
AND LITERATURE

UNIVERSITY OF NORTH CAROLINA
STUDIES IN THE ROMANCE LANGUAGES
AND LITERATURE

THE
ITALIAN QUESTIONE DELLA LINGUA
An Interpretative Essay

Robert A. Hall, Jr.
Brown University

CHAPEL HILL

Copyright 1942
By University of North Carolina
Chapel Hill, N. C.

TABLE OF CONTENTS

PREFACE 1

CHAPTER:

    I. THE PROBLEMS UNDER DISCUSSION 3

    II. EXTERNAL HISTORY OF THE DEBATES 11

    III. WHO WAS RIGHT? 26

    IV. PROGRESS IN SCIENTIFIC METHOD IN THE RENAISSANCE 33

    V. THE SIGNIFICANCE OF THE QUESTIONE DELLA LINGUA 49

APPENDIX:

    I. CHRONOLOGICAL TABLE 57

    II. NOTES AND CITATIONS 62

To

F. A. H.

THE ITALIAN QUESTIONE DELLA LINGUA
by
ROBERT A. HALL, JR.

PREFACE

This essay is an effort to outline briefly the subject-matter and history of the debates on the Italian language, which lasted from Dante's time until the end of the nineteenth century, and which are known in Italy as the Questione della Lingua; and to set forth the relation of these debates to progress in the scientific study of language and to the development of the Italian standard language itself. Our purpose is not to present new material, but rather to give a selective 'interpretazione sintetica' of the general significance of the Questione della Lingua. For this reason, no effort has been made to present a detailed history or minute examination of all the writings involved in the Questione della Lingua; for this type of treatment, the reader is referred to the treatises of Vivaldi, Belardinelli, and Mme. Labande-Jeanroy. For the same reason, attention has been concentrated primarily upon the sixteenth century, in which period the ideas set forth in the debates were first developed and had most vital significance.

The material presented in Chapter IV (Progress in Scientific Method in the Renaissance) is a condensation and revision in essay form of the author's unpublished doctoral thesis, La Filosofia del Linguaggio nel Cinquecento Italiano, presented at the R. Università degli Studi di Roma in 1934. Parts of this material have already appeared, in somewhat different form, under the titles Linguistic Theory in the Italian Renaissance, Language 12.96-107 (1936), and Synchronic Aspects of Renaissance Linguistics, Italica 16.1-11 (1939). Thanks are due to the editors of those journals for permission to reprint this material here, and also to the editors of Studies in Philology for permission to reprint the material contained in Chapter V (The Significance of the Questione della Lingua) from StP 39.1-10 (1942).

The form in which this discussion is presented is that of an essay rather than of a learned monograph. The text is arranged without inset quotations or footnotes, for greater ease of reading, and references—which have been reduced to an absolute minimum—have been placed, as well as a few quotations in the original of passages of fundamental importance, in Appendix II (Notes and Citations). More detailed references and more extensive citations may be found in the three articles mentioned above. A chronological table of the main documents of the Questione della Lingua has been included (as Appendix I) for convenient reference.

The typographical style followed is that of the Linguistic Society of America, as prescribed in its Bulletin no. 14 (1941). Italics are used only for linguistic examples. The abbreviations of periodicals, etc., are those used in the author's Bibliography of Italian Linguistics (Baltimore, 1941).

Thanks are due to the author's colleagues Renato Poggioli and Roger Oake for their kindness in reading the manuscript and making many valuable criticisms and suggestions; and to his wife and parents for their constant help and encouragement.

Chapter 1

The Problems Under Discussion

Before treating the external history of the debates in the Questione della Lingua, it may be desirable to outline briefly the problems which formed the main objects of discussion. These were, in their order of occurrence in the course of the debates: 1. the question of Latin versus Italian; 2. that of purism in its various aspects; and 3. that of orthographical reform. Of these, purism was the most important, and under this inclusive heading may be put the two chief problems of 'Tuscanism' and 'archaism', as well as that of Gallicism in the eighteenth century.

1. LATIN VS. ITALIAN. Shall we write in Latin or in our mother tongue, Italian? This was the problem confronting, at the outset, the writers of mediaeval and Renaissance Italy. In the Middle Ages, the normal popular speech was the local vernacular, but school training and tradition prescribed the use of Latin for literary activity. In the thirteenth century, this tradition had been weakened sufficiently to permit the beginnings of vernacular literature in Italian. In Dante's time the Latin tradition was still strong enough, however, to furnish the occasion for his passionate defence of the use of the mother tongue in the Convivio (1.5-13) and in the De vulgari Eloquentia (especially 1.1.4).

After two centuries of literary use, the vernacular fell, in the fifteenth century, back into a position of relative lack of prestige as contrasted with humanistic Latin. When the use of Italian once more became extensive at the end of the fifteenth century and the beginning of the sixteenth, humanistic scholars manifested opposition to its use. Such humanists as Lazzaro Bonamico, Romolo Amaseo, Francesco Bellofini, and Carlo Sigonio were active in opposing the vernacular. Echos of the discussions which must have been current around the end of the century may be found in Ercole Strozzi's arguments in Bembo's Prose della Volgar Lingua, and in those of Lazzaro (Bonamico) in Speroni's Dialogo delle Lingue. Needless to say, after the first part of the sixteenth century, opposition to the literary use of Italian was slight and devoid of significance; even Romolo Amaseo's oration against the vernacular in 1529 may have been intended mainly as a rhetorical exercise.

2. PURISM, in its essential nature, consists of considering one type of language (a given dialect, or the speech of a given social class or of a certain epoch, etc.) as 'purer' than and therefore 'superior' to other types, and preferable for use in literary endeavor. Under this heading come the several controversies enumerated below:

A. 'TUSCANISM' VS. 'ANTI-TUSCANISM'. It was the contention of a group of critics, whom we shall normally refer to as 'anti-Tuscan', that literary Italian was—or ought to be—based, not on the dialect of Tuscany or on any other regional speech, but on elements common to, and hence taken from, all the dialects of Italy. The first of the 'anti-Tuscans', Dante, described this ideal literary Italian as an 'illustre, cardinale, aulicum et curiale vulgare in Latio, quod omnis latiae civitatis est et nullius esse videtur' (De v. E. 1.16.6). This viewpoint was based on a feeling that no single local dialect, not even Tuscan, was near enough to perfection to be elevated to the dignity of a literary standard, and that, to be truly Italian, the literary language ought to be representative of all Italy. Later, under the attacks of the 'Tuscans' (see below), this party came to deny the Florentine base of standard Italian, and to claim that, because the literary Italian was not absolutely identical with local Florentine usage, and because it contained some non-Florentine or non-Tuscan elements, it was therefore actually a composite such as Dante had set up as an ideal, a true 'italiano comune' or 'volgare illustre' compounded from all the Italian dialects. Some 'anti-Tuscans' even went so far as to deny that Dante, Petrarch, and Boccaccio had written in Florentine or Tuscan at all.

Many critics, however, in the Renaissance and later, were in disagreement with the 'anti-Tuscan' viewpoint, arguing that literary Italian was based on Florentine or Tuscan speech. In support of this contention, they pointed to the identity of Florentine sounds and forms with those of the standard language. This group may be termed 'Tuscans', as they upheld the supremacy of the Florentine or Tuscan dialect in the formation of standard Italian. (Some critics perferred to use the term 'Tuscan' and others 'Florentine' in naming the language; but this was a question of name rather than of essence, and may profitably be disregarded here.) In addition, however, many writers urged also that the Tuscan origin of standard Italian gave Tuscan writers and speakers an authority in linguistic matters which was denied to those of other regions of Italy. Especially when put forward with puristic dogmatism, this assumption of authority led to strong opposition from 'anti-Tuscans'. Some of the latter resorted to disparagement of Tuscan, which they identified with lower-class speech alone and with those residual dialectal features of Tuscan which were not included in literary Italian.

Both 'Tuscan' and 'anti-Tuscan' viewpoints were 'puristic' to a certain degree, in setting up a norm for literary usage which was intended to raise it above the level of local dialectal speech. They differed, however, in the means presumed to be suitable for its establishment. Of these two attitudes, 'Tuscanism' was definitely closer to strict purism, and lent itself more easily to the assumption of superiority and authoritarian prerogatives for one group of speakers over others.

B. 'ARCHAISM' VS. 'ANTI-ARCHAISM'. What stage of the literary language shall we imitate in our writings: the archaic (Trecento) or the modern? This problem came to the fore in the Cinquecento and thereafter, when such a distinction was possible. One group, led by Pietro Bembo, considered that earlier usage, particularly that of Petrarch and Boccaccio and other Trecento writers, was superior to that of modern (Cinquecento) times; they felt that the modern language contained 'impure' elements, whereas the earlier stage of Italian had been 'purified' and had stood the test of time. This theory was supported with doctrines of literary imitation and of the desirability of following models, especially in Bembo's arguments. The conclusion was accordingly reached that later writers should look upon the Trecento as a 'Golden Age' of speech and should imitate its usage—a theory which was sometimes carried to very great extremes, especially by Salviati and the Accademia della Crusca. The critics of this school may accordingly be referred to as 'archaists'.

Other writers, however, did not agree with the high esteem and exclusive supremacy accorded by 'archaistic' theorists to the Trecento in matters of literary usage. The often uncompromisingly puristic attitude of the 'archaists' called forth a strong reaction in favor of modern speech, on the part of many critics, who may consequently be termed 'anti-archaists'. This party asserted that the modern language was not inferior to the earlier, and that it was neither possible nor desirable to limit writers to such words and forms as might have chanced to be used by Petrarch or Boccaccio. It was pointed out, moreover, that Trecento usage was no more 'pure' than that of the Cinquecento, and that many words of the older language had become antiquated and no longer understood, so that their continued use was only an affectation.

Later, during the eighteenth and nineteenth centuries, the works of Cinquecento authors came in their turn to be regarder as 'classics' and to be placed among the models proposed for imitation by the 'archaists'; but the essential division between 'archaists' and their opponents remained the same.

As pointed out by Mme. Labande-Jeanroy in her outstanding treatise on the sixteenth-century Questione della Lingua, any given critic might be on one side in the 'Tuscan' vs. 'anti-Tuscan' dispute, but on the other in that of 'archaism' vs. 'anti-archaism'. In this way, there were four possible combinations, which we give here, together with a few chief exponents of each:

1. 'Tuscan' and 'archaistic' (e.g. Bembo, Salviati, the 'Crusca', Cesari).

2. 'Tuscan' and 'anti-archaistic' (e.g. Machiavelli, Tolomei, Gelli, Giambullari, Varchi, Manzoni).

3. 'Anti-Tuscan' and 'archaistic' (e.g. Muzio).

4. 'Anti-Tuscan' and 'anti-archaistic' (e.g. Calmeta, Equicola, Castiglione, Trissino, Castelvetro, Beni, Cesarotti, Perticari).

Dante, whom many include as a predecessor of the last-mentioned group, was not specifically 'anti-archaistic', as the problem had not yet arisen in his time; but, as he was in favor of the modern tongue—the only vernacular usage in question so far as he was concerned—he may be listed with the 'anti-Tuscan', 'anti-archaistic' school.

C. GALLICISM IN THE EIGHTEENTH CENTURY was a further source of debate, and on the surface appeared to present a new problem. Some authors of the Settecento introduced a great many French loan-words into their works; against this, many protests were made in the name of 'linguistic purity', and considerable controversy arose. This question, however, was really simply a new aspect of the fundamental problem of purism. The 'anti-Gallicists' objected to the flooding of the language by French words, which according to them rendered Italian less 'pure'. The 'Gallicists', as we may term them, replied that the usage of the Trecento, especially, was no freer of impurities than that of modern times (the same argument, it will be noticed, as that advanced by the 'anti-archaists'), and that Mediaeval Italian was particularly replete with French and Provençal loan-words. They further suggested that neologism and foreign borrowings were not only not blameworthy, but necessary to replenish and revivify the vocabulary of the language.

3. ORTHOGRAPHICAL REFORM was in Italy, as in other European countries, a fertile field for debate in the sixteenth century. Several proposals for spelling reform were made, of which the most radical was Trissino's unsuccessful attempt to introduce the use of Greek epsilon and omega to indicate the open varieties of *e* and *o*, and of Greek sigma and zeta for voiced *s* and *z* (i.e. the sounds [z] and [dz]) respectively. Other attempts were made, somewhat more successfully, to eliminate useless *h* (as in *havere* 'avere' etc.) and to distinguish consonantal *i* and *u* by using the letters *j* and *v*. As the divergence of Italian orthography from the actual phonemes of Italian was not great, however, this phase of the debates was not long lived, and scarcely lasted beyond the middle of the sixteenth century.

The subjects outlined above were, of course, not the only ones brought into the discussion by the debaters. Many other considerations, some connected with language and some not at all, were introduced, and were frequently fused and confused with the main issues under discussion. Of these, the chief problems more or less connected with linguistic matters were: 1. an infinite number of grammatical points and disputes about 'correctness', deriving from the sixteenth-century efforts to codify Italian grammar, and 2. considerations of social levels as reflected in language. In this latter connection, 'Tuscans' and 'anti-Tuscans' alike almost always condemned the language of 'l'infima plebe e la feccia del popolazzo', in Varchi's words, confusing the merits of the speakers of a language with those of the language itself.

Many matters wholly unrelated to linguistic problems were also introduced into the debates, especially in the Cinquecento. Political considerations—regret for the fall of the Roman Empire and hatred of invaders, especially Germans—led many, particularly among the humanists, to condemn Italian for its supposed origin from the fusion of Latin and barbarian (Germanic) speech. Religious controversy entered into such cases as the Castelvetro-Caro quarrel and Muzio's infusion of pro-Catholic polemic into his attacks on his opponents. Historical fantasy played a part in the ascription of the origin of Italian to Greek, Etruscan, Hebrew or other sources. Purely aesthetic factors—beauty, 'euphony', personal likes and dislikes—played a great part in determining many critics' preferences, especially among the more puristically inclined.

Needless to say, the debaters themselves did not always analyze the Questione della Lingua into its component parts, or distinguish the various aspects of the discussion as we have tried to do above. In fact, they mingled non-essentials with essentials so frequently, and often in so great a proportion, as to cause some later historians to regard the whole Questione della Lingua as a 'wearisome, perpetually recurrent quarrel about words' (Symonds) or as 'des querelles de pédants' (Labande-Jeanroy). In order to avoid this excessive attitude of depreciation, and to distinguish the really valuable and original work done by some critics and writers in the Questione della Lingua, we must carefully separate the wheat from the chaff, and concentrate our attention upon the positive results attained during the discussions. This, after outlining briefly the external history of the debates, we shall attempt to do in the following chapters.

Chapter II
External History of the Debates

In this chapter we shall attempt to give a brief résumé of the development of the Questione della Lingua in chronological order, and to discuss the main documents and the debates to which they gave rise. As this section is intended to be only a brief survey, we shall take no account of minor authors or polemics, and our attention will be concentrated primarily on the Cinquecento, the period in which the lines of the discussion were first drawn. For detailed history of the discussions, reference may be made to the works of Vivaldi, Belardinelli, and Mme. Labande-Jeanroy.

1. DANTE was the first to write extensively on the problem of the standard language. His De vulgari Eloquentia (usually dated ca. 1305) was the first document in the Questione della Lingua, and the source of many of the theories of the 'anti-Tuscan' school. The first book is divided into two main sections, of which the first begins with a general discussion of linguistic theory (1.1), a scholastic demonstration of the restriction of speech to man alone and the reasons therefor (1.2, 3), and a brief historical discussion of the development of human speech, in which Dante follows biblical tradition as his main authority (1.4-7). In this connection, Dante is the first theorist on language to recognize change as an inevitable characteristic of human speech. Dante then surveys briefly the speech of Europe, establishing a tripartite division of tongues, and distinguishing essentially the Greek, Germanic, and Romance families; and among the Romance languages, he establishes a further tripartite division, according to the affirmative particle: the languages of *oc, oil,* and *sì,* i.e. Provençal, French,

and Italian (1.8-9). Latin is conceived of as having been established by convention in order to provide an immutable language free from the continual change inevitable in ordinary speech; whether Italian derived from Latin or not is not specifically decided.

The second half of the first book deals with the nature and literary merits of the Italian dialects (1.10-15). Dante enumerates the fourteen dialects which he distinguishes, seven on each side of the Apennines, and then proceeds to cite examples from each and to pass judgment on their worth. He concludes that, on aesthetic and moral grounds, none of them is fit for use as a literary language in the noble genres. Bolognese and Sicilian are the only dialects which find even a degree of favor; Tuscan receives especially severe condemnation. Searching for a noble literary language in which the highest forms of literature may be written, Dante then deduces that such a language exists, not in any one of the local dialects of Italy, but over and above all of them, in elements (primarily of vocabulary) common to all the dialects (1.16-19). The extant part of the second book passes then to a discussion of poetical types and meters, in the midst of which it breaks off.

The De vulgari Eloquentia is an isolated monument in the Questione della Lingua, which is thereafter quiescent, to all intents and purposes, for approximately two centuries. We know of no contemporary discussion of Dante's theories or answer to the De vulgari Eloquentia. Passing mention is made by various writers of the Trecento (Boccaccio, Sacchetti, Francesco da Barberino, Antonio da Tempo, and others) of Tuscan speech as the language of literary usage, but they devote no attention to discussion of fundamental principles or theoretical aspects of their practice in linguistic matters. This situation continued through the fifteenth century under the dominance of Latin humanism.

The famous Bruni-Biondo debate, of 1435, is worthy of mention as having a bearing on the Renaissance conception of the origin of Italian and its relation to Latin. Leonardo Bruni maintained that the plebeian speech of ancient Rome must have been very close to modern Italian, and as a consequence quite different from Classical Latin, so that there was, in his conception, a wide gulf between upper- and lower-class Latin speech. According to this theory, the language of oratory and the theater must have been well-nigh incomprehensible to the proletarians. This interpretation of the nature of the sermo plebeius was answered by Biondo, who pointed out, with arguments based on evidence from Classical times, that, despite the existence of certain differences between vulgar and elegant speech, there was essential unity in Latin usage, and that the present form of modern Italian was due to a development out of Latin in the course of time. The significance of this debate is that it represents a certain point at which the doctrine of linguistic change was just beginning to spread, but had not penetrated to the minds of all. Bruni's theory implies the old attitude, lacking any conception of change in linguistic structure, so that it was possible for him to conceive of plebeian Latin as having lasted on, substantially unchanged, for fifteen hundred years into contemporary times. Biondo's attitude, on the other hand, takes into account the possibility of linguistic evolution, and therefore shows more historical perspicacity. Bruni's doctrine of the identity of plebeian Latin with Italian failed to receive acceptance in later epochs, except for sporadic revivals by such men as Castelvetro, F. di Diano, and Gravina.

2. THE RENAISSANCE. With the Cinquecento, however, and the resurgence of Italian as the national literary language, supported by the movement towards 'umanesimo volgare' or humanism in the vernacular, the questions outlined in Chapter I came to the fore, and the debates on the subject were almost endless.

The first outbreak of polemic came in connection with the 'anti-Tuscan' movement, which first appeared in the Cinquecento under the guise of a doctrine favoring the use of a 'courtly' type of speech ('lingua cortigiana'), instead of one more narrowly Tuscan. This 'lingua cortigiana' was supposed to represent the usage prevailing at the courts of Italy, especially the papal court. Its characteristics were somewhat ill-defined, but, if we may take the precepts and style of Castiglione's Cortegiano as representative, it seems to have consisted primarily in a greater receptivity towards current fashionable usage, dialectal forms, Latinisms, and Iberisms than would have been permitted by strict adherence to Tuscan forms alone. This doctrine was said to have been presented first by Vincenzo Calmeta in a book written in the first decade of the sixteenth century, Della Lingua cortigiana. Unfortunately, this book has been lost (according to Castelvetro, deliberately destroyed in manuscript by Varchi), and so we are forced to rely on second-hand description for an account of Calmeta's theories. It must have contained, however, a discussion of 'courtly' usage, and recommendations for its preference to Tuscan or archaic authority. Much the same point of view was presented by Mario Equicola in his Della natura di amore (first part of the sixteenth century; definitive edition, 1525), in which precepts were laid down for the pleasing and agreeable use of courtly speech in elegant society. Castiglione's Cortegiano (published 1528, but written, especially the first part, considerably earlier) contains, in several passages of the first book, what is possibly the most detailed presentation extant of the doctrine of the 'lingua cortigiana'. A somewhat generalized Italian is recommended as a model, and specifically Tuscan idiom—identified, as it was by many of the 'anti-Tuscans', with uneducated or rustic usage—and antiquated expressions come in for some humorous condemnation.

The first important reply to these theories came in the Prose della volgar Lingua of Pietro Bembo (written early in the sixteenth century; published 1525). A lengthy dialogue in four books, the Prose della volgar Lingua open with a discussion of the relative merits of Latin and Italian. Ercole Strozzi, the humanist, upholds the superiority of Latin, using also Bruni's old theory to demonstrate the inferiority of the 'volgare', but he is argued down by the other speakers. Then, presenting his own views through the utterances in the dialogue of his brother Carlo, Bembo proceeds to justify the 'Tuscan' and 'archaistic' point of view. Bembo shows that standard Italian has a Tuscan base, and argues further that, in order to use this language best in literature, one should set up norms for imitation, choosing the best writers of earlier times—i.e. Petrarch and Boccaccio—as models. Through this book and his personal influence, Bembo became the leader of the 'puristic' school in language and literature, which became dominant in most fields by the end of the century. The Prose della volgar Lingua have a place in the history of Italian grammar as well, through the detailed discussion and outline of Italian morphology which Bembo introduces, thus rendering them, however, somewhat topheavy with grammatical analysis.

Another reply to the partisans of the 'lingua cortigiana', and possibly the most effective one, was given in the Dialogo intorno alla nostra Lingua (ca. 1514) of Machiavelli. In this brief and trenchant analysis of the problem, the writer points out irrefutably the close concordance of standard Italian with Florentine not only in vocabulary, but also in phonetic and morphological structure. He ends the discussion by calling up the spirit of Dante, and forcing Dante to admit that the Divine Comedy was written in Florentine, not some kind of 'italiano comune', notwithstanding the presence of some loan-words in the Commedia.

The interest in a national standard language led some scholars to perceive that Italian orthography was not wholly satisfactory, and to attempt to reform it. The best known of these efforts was Gian Giorgio Trissino's ill-fated attempt to introduce Greek letters, as described in the previous chapter. This reform he defended in his Letter to Pope Clement VII (1524), prefixed to the edition of his tragedy Sofonisba, and referring to his desire to provide exact representation for standard Italian: 'Considerando io la pronunzia italiana ... ' etc. Trissino's proposed reforms called forth a storm of protest, and several attacks, by A. Firenzuola, L. Martelli, and C. Tolomei (under two pseudonyms), soon appeared in rapid succession. Of these polemic replies to Trissino, all but the dialogue Il Polito (published by Tolomei under the pseudonym of A. Franci) are simply ill-tempered efforts to ridicule an unwelcome novelty. Il Polito, however, represents a more constructive type of criticism. Tolomei points out, with arguments based on a sound knowledge of phonetics, the further needs for orthographical reform, and the partial and unsatisfactory nature of Trissino's proposal.

As an outcome of this polemic, Trissino published in 1529 a translation of Dante's De vulgari Eloquentia, whose position he made his own, maintaining that standard Italian was in fact what Dante proclaimed it ought to be in theory: a composite language containing elements drawn from all the local dialects of the peninsula. Some 'Tuscans', not liking the ascription of these arguments to Dante, attempted to disprove the authenticity of the De vulgari Eloquentia; whereupon Trissino, in answer to these and other criticisms, wrote and published his dialogue Il Castellano (1529). In this he puts into the mouth of his spokesman, the Castellano Rucellai, a defense of the 'anti-Tuscan' position, bolstered up by pseudo-philosophical arguments.

The year 1529 is interesting also because of the oration delivered in that year by the humanist Romolo Amaseo, attacking the use of the vernacular and upholding the merits of humanistic Latin. This is practically the last serious defense of Latin with which we meet, in the literary field at least.

Speroni's Dialogo delle Lingue, composed in 1530 or soon after, presents an interesting picture of the debates current at that time, without, however, giving us a clear-cut decision as to the author's own stand on the subject. A dialogue within a dialogue, it recounts first a debate between a humanist (Messer Lazzaro), a courtier, and Cardinal Bembo, on the merits of Italian versus Latin, and of 'courtly' (modern) versus Trecento usage. Into this dialogue is inserted another, narrated by a student as having taken place between Peretto (Pomponazzi, the philosopher) and the humanist Lascaris, in which Peretto maintains the equal value of all languages and dialects, at least for scientific and philosophical use. (This equalitarian position in linguistic matters was especially radical for the Cinquecento, with all its wide-spread social and intellectual prejudices.) Speroni seems to give the victory to Peretto in the second debate, but in the first to Bembo and his puristic doctrines as applied to literary usage.

In this period also, whether around 1525 or around 1535, was written one of the outstanding defenses of the 'Tuscan' but 'anti-archaistic' point of view, Tolomei's dialogue Il Cesano. In this we find an essentially sound and well-balanced presentation of the reasons for considering standard Italian as based on Tuscan, and for taking the living language as the model for literary use. Here, also, as in others of Tolomei's writings more specifically concerned with formal grammar, we find some of the most striking anticipations of scientific assumptions in linguistic method that are to be found in the sixteenth century (see below, chapter IV).

A follower of Trissino, but rather more archaizing and puristic in his inclinations, Girolamo Muzio published during the years from 1530 to 1536 various letters and opuscules, which were later gathered together and published as his Battaglie in difesa dell' italica lingua. They are chiefly valuable as showing clearly that the viewpoints of 'Tuscanism' and 'purism' were by no means synonymous, and that it was possible for such a writer as Muzio to combine the 'anti-Tuscan' viewpoint of Trissino with an uncompromising purism and authoritarian attitude in linguistic matters.

Towards the middle of the century, although writers on the matter of the standard language were still divided as to its 'Tuscan' or 'non-Tuscan' nature, the question of 'archaism' began to occupy the center of the stage. The works of the two Florentine writers, G. B. Gelli (I Capricci del Bottaio; Discorso sopra la difficoltà di ordinare la lingua di Firenze) and P. F. Giambullari (Il Gello), present the 'Tuscan' viewpoint, but argue in favor of considerable freedom for writers in using the modern tongue. Gelli, in fact, argues that it is not possible to set down fixed rules as yet, since Florentine speech, far from having reached its state of perfection in the Trecento, is still in a state of flux and has yet to attain its highest point. In his Capricci del Bottaio, Gelli has some interesting observations defending individual liberty in linguistic usage and the necessity of neologism for enriching a language, which are set forth to Giusto the cobbler by his soul.

Another defense of Tuscan and modern usage is to be found in the extremely long-winded but thorough discussion given by Benedetto Varchi in his dialogue L'Ercolano (before 1565; published 1570). In this work, Varchi narrates through the mouth of another a series of conversations between himself and the Conte Ercolani, in which Varchi expounds all his theories on the nature of speech in general and of standard Italian, as equivalent to modern spoken Florentine, in particular. The first full answer to the doctrines expounded by Trissino in the Castellano, Varchi's Ercolano is particularly significant by reason of the attention given to the spoken language as the source of literary expression; but like the Castellano, it is marred by a number of abstract, pseudo-philosophical considerations which detract from rather than add to the argument.

Lodovico Castelvetro, an acute but excessively polemical critic, had already entered into the debates on the language with his severe criticisms of Caro's poem 'Venite all'ombra de' gran gigli d'oro', which provoked a very long and bitter quarrel (1553 ff.). Castelvetro was also the author of a series of Giunte alle Prose del Bembo (written during the 1550's). This work contains some very keen and justified criticisms of Bembo's theories and statements, but also, unfortunately, some attacks made out of pure contrariness, such as Castelvetro's revival of Bruni's old theory of Italian as being equivalent to the sermo plebeius of ancient Rome. Castelvetro also made a severe criticism of Varchi's Ercolano in his Correzione di alcune cose nel dialogo delle lingue di M. B. Varchi (1573). In the Correzione, Castelvetro attacks Varchi's 'Tuscanism', and also criticizes Varchi for his lack of understanding of scientific method, by the use of which some of Varchi's objections to etymology as a science might be answered.

Girolamo Muzio also criticized the Ercolano, in his polemic work La Varchina (written in 1573). Whereas Castelvetro has criticized Varchi from an 'anti-Tuscan' and scientific point of view, Muzio based his attack upon 'anti-Tuscan' and puristic grounds, condemning Varchi for his acceptance of contemporary usage and the spoken language as a norm.

The remaining disputes during the Cinquecento may be passed over, as contributing nothing essentially new to the controversy. The outstanding polemic of the end of the sixteenth century was that occasioned by Salviati's puristic and pedantic attack upon Tasso in his Stacciate contro la Gerusalemme Liberata (1585), and his further exposition of puristic doctrine in the Avvertimenti della lingua sopra il Decamerone. Answers to Salviati's uncalled-for attacks on Tasso were soon forthcoming, and the debate lasted well into the seventeenth century.

At the end of the Cinquecento and beginning of the Seicento, several works on historical Italian grammar were published by Celso Cittadini, who derived Florentine speech from the popular speech of Rome, but made due allowance for historical development. Cittadini was at one time thought to have been the true originator of scientific historical grammar in Italy; it was shown by Sensi, however, that he derived his method from Tolomei, so, although Cittadini cannot be termed a plagiarist, his work does not represent such an advance in method as does Tolomei's.

3. THE SEVENTEENTH AND EIGHTEENTH CENTURIES. In these centuries, although from time to time new occasions for debate arose and new polemics broke out, the viewpoints taken and arguments advanced remained essentially the same. In the following, therefore, we shall not discuss the Seicento and Settecento debates on the language in such detail as we have for the Cinquecento, but shall limit our discussion to the few main debates during the later period.

Soon after the beginning of the seventeenth century, the first edition of the Vocabulary of the Accademia della Crusca, edited according to very strict 'Tuscan' and puristic principles, began to appear. During the seventeenth and eighteenth centuries, the Crusca continued to exert a powerful influence on behalf of narrow purism and antiquarianism. This policy of the Crusca, and its embodiment in the Vocabulary, called forth a deluge of criticism. Some 'anti-Tuscans' attacked the Vocabulary; of these the most important were Alessandro Tassoni (in his Pensieri Diversi, 1612) and Paolo Beni, who undertook to criticize the Crusca in his Anticrusca (1612). To this latter, polemic replies were made by Orlando Pescetti and Benedetto Fioretti. Beni continued the war on purism in his reply (published under the pseudonym of Michelangelo Fonte) Il Cavalcante, an attack on Pescetti, the Crusca, and Salviati; he also wrote in 1616 a special defense of Tasso in his Commento sulla Gerusalemme Liberata. Some 'Tuscans' as well, as including Cittadini, condemned the excessively archaistic doctrines of the Crusca and its vocabulary, which continued to be a storm centre, in its successive editions, for some time.

Various defenses of the 'Tuscan' viewpoint were published during the seventeenth century, some maintaining the strictly puristic attitude of the Crusca, such as those of Pescetti and Fioretti and others in their replies to Beni, and of Carlo Dati in his Dell' obbligo di ben parlar la propria lingua (1657). Others, somewhat more liberal, admitted the possibility of 'error' in the Trecentisti and of merit in modern usage, as did D. Bartoli in his Il Torto e il Diritto del Non si può (1655-68).

These debates lasted on into the eighteenth century; we may cite in the early eighteenth century, as examples of the 'Tuscan' puristic stand, A. M. Salvini's Discorsi accademici (1695) and Prose toscane (1715), A. M. Biscioni's Note al Malmantile (1731), and N. Amenta's Della lingua nobile d'Italia (1723). A curious example of 'Tuscan' but anti-puristic and even anti-Florentine attitude is Girolamo Gigli's defense of Sienese in his Dizionario cateriniano (1717). An interesting 'anti-Tuscan' document is Arizzi's comedy Il toscanismo e la Crusca (1739).

As the eighteenth century passed, the question of purism came to be connected with that of French influence on the Italian language and the reaction against it. The importation of French ideas and words aroused a strong opposition, at first among the ultra-purists, and then among others like Parini who were desirous of counteracting French influence. Among those favoring French borrowings may be mentioned Bettinelli, Zanotti, Algarotti and Denina; among the purists, Corticelli and Parini. The division into 'anti-Tuscan' and 'Tuscan' continued; the ranks of the 'anti-Tuscans' included Fontanini, Muratori, Zanotti, Alessandro Conti, A. and P. Verri, Appiano Buonafede, and Tiraboschi, whereas among the 'Tuscans', in addition to Salvini and Biscioni may be mentioned G. C. Becelli (an ultra-purist, as shown in his Se oggidì, scrivendo, si debba usare la lingua italiana del buon secolo, published 1737) and Algarotti.

The outstanding document of the Questione della Lingua in the Settecento is undoubtedly Melchiorre Cesarotti's Saggio sulla filosofia della lingue (1785). This essay, in four sections, is a skillful presentation of the anti-puristic, 'anti-Tuscan' point of view. After a general introduction, in which he combats certain prevalent errors (such ideas as the natural superiority of one type of speech over another, or concepts such as purity, logic, authority, perfection, inalterability, uniformity, as applied to language), he proceeds in the second and third books to a detailed examination of the use of language and its various aspects as a literary medium, and to a philosophical justification of freedom, and, where necessary, innovation, in its treatment. In the final chapter, Cesarotti emphasizes the fact that standard Italian, even though closest to Florentine and helped to its greatness especially by Florentine authors, is now the possession of the entire Italian nation, who therefore, according to his argument, have a right to share in determining its use and contributing to its enrichment. After expressing the desire to see the Italian dialects cultivated more as literary media, Cesarotti proposes to replace the narrow, Tuscan-dominated authority of the Accademia della Crusca with that of a body of literary men of all Italy, to provide more liberal guidance and direction for the literary language.

4. THE NINETEENTH CENTURY. Cesarotti's Saggio is the last document of creative criticism to which the Questione della Lingua gave rise. The Questione itself lasted on, however, nearly a hundred years more. The quarrel between purists and anti-purists continued unabated. Among the

conservatives may be mentioned Antonio Cesari (who, in his various publications, simply continued the viewpoint of Bembo and the 'Tuscan' purists) and his followers, and Basilio Puoti. The opposition to ultra-purism was led by Vincenzo Monti (especially in his Proposta di alcune correzioni ed aggiunte al Vocabolario della Crusca, in seven volumes, 1817-1826), G. Perticari, G. Barbieri, and others. Polemics were especially vigorous at the time of the appearance of the successive volumes of Monti's Proposta.

Alessandro Manzoni is usually credited with having played a decisive role in effecting the ultimate cessation of the Questione della Lingua with the victory of the Tuscan but non-archaistic viewpoint. This accomplishment is usually ascribed, not so much to his theoretical utterances on the linguistic problem, as to the efficacy of his example in revising the language of his Promessi Sposi to conform more exactly to contemporary Florentine usage. It must be noted, however, that there were, at the same time, several other factors involved whose ultimate cogency was greater than that of even a very popular and influential novel, especially political factors.

G. I. Ascoli's Proemio to the Archivio Glottologico (1872) may be considered the last important document on the 'anti-Tuscan' side. In this he points out, with corroboration from his extensive knowledge of linguistic science and method, that the linguistic conditions in Italy were not the same as those in France and other European countries where a powerful centralizing influence had been at work, and that hence, through the collaboration and contribution of many non-Tuscans, standard Italian was no longer the exclusive property of Florence or Tuscany.

After 1870, the desire in Italy for unification was fulfilled, and with political unification came a greater exertion of linguistic influence of the capital (first Florence and then Rome, whose speech had by the nineteenth century come to be assimilated to the Central Italian type, fairly close to that of Florence). Universal education and military training had a further effect in spreading the knowledge of Tuscan as the standard language; in more recent times, there have been the further unifying forces of talking pictures and radio. With further progress towards the achievement of linguistic unification, the Questione della Lingua died a natural death. A few ill-timed attempts have been made to revive debate, but without success. In Migliorini's Lingua Contemporanea (1939) we find the Questione della Lingua treated, as it should be, as a thing of the past. The problems confronting the Italian language at present are no longer the traditional ones of the Questione della Lingua, but those facing the standard language of the nation as a whole.

Chapter III
Who Was Right?

Later historians, in dealing with the Questione della Lingua, have frequently been inclined to take sides with one or the other of the parties, according to their own predilections. Thus Symonds expressed approval of Castiglione's doctrines of 'courtly' speech, because of his own dislike of pedantic purism. Belardinelli sympathized with the theories of Muzio and the 'anti-Tuscans' because of the broader 'national' viewpoint implied in their philosophy, and decried the excessively separatistic devotion shown to their local dialect by the 'Tuscans'. Mme. Labande-Jeanroy's sympathy with the puristic viewpoint, on the other hand, led her to approve only of the 'Tuscan' party.

The present-day critic is inclined to recognize the need of impartiality and to hesitate in taking sides as freely as past historians have done. Yet we recognize the desirability of examining critically the arguments of the various parties in the debates, in order to aid the reader to form a critical judgment of their relative value. In the following, therefore, we shall attempt to evaluate the several theories presented in the debates, and the only viewpoint allowed to influence our conclusions will be that of modern linguistic science.

1. 'TUSCANS' OR 'ANTI-TUSCANS'? Most historians, especially of Italian literature, have been inclined to say, diplomatically, that there is 'much to be said on both sides'. Symonds and Belardinelli, as pointed out above favored the 'anti-Tuscans'; Mme. Labande-Jeanroy, on the other hand, categorically asserts that the 'Tuscans' alone were right. In order to clarify the situation, however, we must distinguish between three elements of the disagreement: the ori-

gin and nature of Italian, its extension, and the question of authority.

A. THE ORIGIN AND NATURE OF ITALIAN was asserted by the 'Tuscans' to be Tuscan; the 'anti-Tuscans' denied either this origin or its relevance. So far as the actual origin and nature of standard Italian is concerned, we must agree with Mme. Labande-Jeanroy and say that the 'Tuscan' party was right. Standard Italian has a Tuscan base; this fact is not impaired on the one hand, by the presence of some Latinisms, dialectal borrowings, or loan-words in standard Italian, nor, on the other hand, by slight divergences between Florentine vernacular and standard Italian. Modern linguistics furnishes incontrovertible proofs of the Tuscan, and more specifically Florentine, nature of standard Italian. Among these proofs may be mentioned such features as: 1. the suffix *-aio* from *-ariu*, as opposed to *-aro* or similar developments in other dialects; 2. the change of Vulgar Latin close *e* to *i* before *n* plus guttural (as in *fingo, lingua*) and the corresponding change of close *o* to *u* (*unghia, fungo*), as opposed to *e, o* in these positions elsewhere; 3. the absence of umlaut (influence of the final vowel upon the tonic), which is very widespread in both northern and southern Italy; 4. the suffix *-iamo* in the first person plural of verbs, as opposed to *-amo -emo -imo* elsewhere in Italy; etc.

B. THE EXTENSION OF STANDARD ITALIAN reached, by the sixteenth century, to the upper classes throughout Italy, in the cultural centers at least. Now whenever a given dialect is extended over a whole country or region, in its spread it always takes up certain features from the dialects which it overlays or supersedes; thus standard French (based on the speech of the Ile-de-France, or Francien) has certain non-Parisian or non-Francien features (*amour, abeille*), and likewise with standard Spanish, English, etc.

This same process took place in the spread of standard Italian, with the borrowing in to the standard language of words from non-Tuscan dialects. At the same time, certain features characteristic of the original local dialect are usually lost during its spread, and are not present in the koiné or standard language thus formed. This also took place in the formation of standard Italian, and some local idioms of Florentine or Tuscan speech (often referred to in the debates as 'arzigogoli' or 'riboboli') failed to find a place in the generalized koiné.

In this connection, both the 'Tuscans' and the 'anti-Tuscans' usually failed to see the truth of the matter, which in this case actually did lie somewhat between the extreme of the positions adopted. The 'Tuscan' party usually exaggerated in the direction of narrowness, not being willing to admit the permissibility of non-Tuscan elements in literary Italian (at any rate, such non-Tuscan elements as were of recent origin and had not been consecrated by use in the literary classics). Such purists as Salviati and the 'Crusca' group refused to admit that standard Italian could ever be anything except pure Tuscan, and treated even the generalized Italian of non-Tuscans as fundamentally different from and inferior to Tuscan. This attitude was facilitated by the political divisions in Italy during the Renaissance and later, which made it possible to exaggerate the differences between 'pure' Tuscan and the standard Italian spoken in, say, Milan or Venice, as being equal in order to differences between national languages.

The 'anti-Tuscan' party, in answer to this attitude of superiority taken by the 'Tuscans', frequently exaggerated the differences in another way. To emphasize the fact that standard Italian was now the common possession of all Italians, and as such slightly different from local Tuscan, would have been the most sensible answer, and is in fact the position taken by Cesarotti and other temperate 'anti-Tuscans'. Others, however, such as Trissino and his followers, went much farther, and to uphold their assertion that standard Italian was not identical with Tuscan, took the untenable position that Tuscan was only that residue of local speech which was not included in standard Italian.

A further argument introduced by the 'anti-Tuscans' into the debates, and one which has served to becloud the issue greatly, was the assertion, first made by Trissino, that the 'volgare illustre' or 'aulico' set up by Dante was actually a fact, and that literary Italian was really such a compound dialect, made up of elements common to all the dialects of Italy. Now the plain truth of the matter is that such a 'volgare aulico' never existed, outside of the imagination of Dante and the 'anti-Tuscans'. This exalted literary language was set up by Dante as an ideal in the De vulgari Eloquentia; but his own practice in the Divina Commedia, and even in the Vita Nuova, was definitely at odds with his theory. He did not take elements from all the Italian dialects and form an artificial compound speech, but he based his usage on that of Florence. (Machiavelli's trenchant demonstration of this should have sufficed for all following generations.) The further formation of standard Italian in the Trecento, and its spread in the successive centuries, was of the same type as that of standard French, Spanish, or English, as pointed out above; standard Italian was never a language formed by artificial compounding, like Church Slavonic or the Landsmaal in Norway.

C. THE QUESTION OF AUTHORITY goes beyond the realm of fact into that of privilege. The 'Tuscan' party claimed that the Tuscan origin and nature of standard Italian gave the speakers of Tuscan the right to act as authorities in linguistic matters, and to prescribe for the other speakers of standard Italian what they should or should not say, in accordance with strict Tuscan usage. For non-Tuscan speakers of the standard language, the natural reaction to this attitude was to question the right of the 'Tuscans' to assume such an exclusive privilege, and to assert their own equal rights in decisions concerning usage.

In this matter, we must conclude that the 'anti-Tuscan' party was nearer the truth than the 'Tuscans'. Linguistic science has substantiated the opinion of Peretto Pomponazzi in Speroni's Dialogo, that no type of linguistic structure and no linguistic phenomenon is inherently and inalterably superior to any other. Nor does any speaker of a language have any inherent authority over any other speaker. Such authority as a speaker may appear to have comes to him only through the desire of others to imitate him, and this desire always comes from a wish to obtain his favor because of his dominance in some non-linguistic respect: political or economic power, social prestige, or the like. In this case, once a standard language based on Tuscan had spread outside of Tuscany, any speaker who acquired that language (whether in his family or in school) had fully as much 'right of possession' over it as the inhabitants of the region where it originated; he might therefore regard himself as having as much authority in the use he made of it as anyone else, and in the introduction of loan-words from his own dialect, in neologisms, and the like, to suit his own needs.

2. 'ARCHAISTS' OR 'ANTI-ARCHAISTS'? In this connection, it is well to make a distinction at the outset between literary and non-literary usage. For the attainment of specific artistic aims, the writer of literature, especially poetry, must often depend upon effects produced on his hearer by the

use either of customary forms in unaccustomed ways, or else of unaccustomed (usually archaic, exotic, or otherwise unfamiliar) forms. These latter, particularly, bring to the hearer associations and suggestions different from those of ordinary speech. Hence, if any given school of writers wish to limit themselves in their activity to any specific aspect of the linguistic material with which they are working, be it archaic or any other, they are at liberty to do so in their own work.

Trouble arises, however, when theorists wish to extend to ordinary speech and writing the criteria and limitations which are set up for individual school of artistic endeavor. Here again, linguistic science has shown us that Peretto's position is essentially correct; it is not possible to declare that any stage of a language is 'better' than any other. In the words of Giusto the cobbler's soul, in Gelli's Capricci, 'all languages....are fit to express the ideas and needs of their speakers; and even if they be otherwise, then their speakers made them fit', i. e. by borrowing and new formation. Purists in all speech-communities frequently object to these means of enriching the vocabulary; but the objections made are normally based on aesthetic, political, social, or similar considerations necessarily invalid from a scientific point of view. The same may be said of problems of 'correctness' in grammatical details.

Hence, aside from consideration of literary preference, which do not concern us here, we must conclude that the 'anti-archaists' were in the right in protesting against the effort of the 'archaists' to impose upon standard Italian the limitation, originating in Bembo's and the Neo-Platonists' doctrines of literary imitation, to old-time or established usage alone. Many archaic forms naturally became antiquated in later periods, and on the other hand new facts, situations, and theories arose which called for new nomenclature. In this—which is in most speech communities the normal—situation, current usage, supplemented by borrowing and new formation as necessary, was of course preferable.

The same considerations apply to the quarrel between 'Gallicizers' and purists in the eighteenth century, and we must conclude that the latters' objections were unfounded.

3. THE RESPONSIBILITY OF THE PURISTS in aggravating and protracting the Questione della Lingua must be recognized as the surface cause of its excessive duration; in the last chapter, we shall consider the underlying conditions which rendered this possible. It will be noticed that, in general, the puristic element (mostly the 'Tuscans' and the 'archaists') were more inclined towards narrow-mindedness than their opponents, more aggressive, more authoritarian, and (except in the question of fact concerning the historical origin of Italian) more nearly in the wrong. If critics like Salviati, the Crusca and its defenders, and Cesari had not persisted in claiming excessive privileges for Tuscan and archaic usage, the excessive opposition and misunderstanding of the basic nature of the standard language would not have arisen.

Chapter IV

Progress In Scientific Method In the Renaissance

Although a great proportion of the debates in the Questione della Lingua were, in the last analysis, caused by the excessive zeal of purists, and could to a considerable extent have been avoided, nevertheless we must not fall into the error of dismissing the entire Questione della Lingua as meaningless or unimportant. As by-products of the quarrels, and in order to provide material for argument, numerous points of general theory and philosophy of language and linguistic change were developed in the course of the debates in the Cinquecento. In many respects, the theories developed during the Renaissance mark a considerable advance over the notions which had prevailed in previous centuries. A number of Renaissance concepts were developed 'at home' with intelligent and fruitful use of the available data, and anticipate (in germ, at least) by three centuries developments ordinarily ascribed to the nineteenth century and to acquaintanceship with Hindu grammarians' methods.

We shall here outline briefly, therefore, the advances and improvements in linguistic theory which were made in the course of the debates, under the heads, first of language considered as a social phenomenon, and then of linguistic analysis treated from both the synchronic (descriptive) and the diachronic (historical) points of view.

1. LANGUAGE AS A SOCIAL PHENOMENON. The nature of language itself was not usually summarized very far beyond a general formula such as that of Varchi: 'Il parlare, ovvero favellare umano, non è altro che manifestare ad alcuno i

concetti dell' animo mediante le parole'. In regard to the 'natural' or 'artificial' origin of words (a favorite subject for debate in the linguistic philosophy of antiquity) the Scholastics' synthesis of the old so-called 'Platonic' and 'Aristotelian' viewpoints, which had been expressed by Dante in the well-known passage in Paradiso 26.130-132, continued to be accepted throughout the Cinquecento in Varchi's and others' support of the ad placitum doctrine, with only a few unimportant exceptions. (Castelvetro revived the theory that words had a 'natural' origin, i.e. some inherent relation to the objects denoted, but only to contradict Bembo; Vico, at a later date, revived it to accord with his philosophy of language.) The same is true of the traditional view of the connection between language and thought, conceived of as being quite loose, and language and thought as being easily separable and distinct. This dualism corresponds to that prevalent in other fields of philosophy and aesthetics in the Renaissance.

A. INDIVIDUAL DIFFERENCES IN SPEECH, however, were recognized from Dante's time onward, more so than they ever had been before. This applies not only to differences between speech-communities, but also between individuals. The best-known passage concerning individual differences is that in Trissino's Castellano, where it is pointed out that even members of the same family may show divergences in their speech, and of course different families may have peculiarities which set their usage off from others'. This recognition of the individual as the prime linguistic unity was a general Renaissance concept, and not merely limited to the 'anti-Tuscan' group, as Mme. Labande-Jeanroy has asserted; for in 'Tuscan' writers as well, such as Tolomei in his Cesano, and Varchi in the Ercolano, we frequently find similar statements. Varchi, in fact, even uses existence of individual variations and differences in pronunciation to combat Trissino's use of the term 'Italian pronunciation'.

B. LANGUAGE AND 'SOCIAL ORGANISM'. But neither Trissino, an 'anti-Tuscan', nor Varchi, a 'Tuscan', for example, were willing to grant any importance to this recognition of the individual differences in speech, since both of them wished to take into account only dialectal differences. Trissino justified himself in this with a philosophical consideration, that of the impossibility of descending below the 'specie specialissima'; and Varchi protests in one place against what is essentially his own recognition of individual differences. At another point he goes farther still, and declares that to be a true language, a linguistic system must be used not only by any given group of persons, but by an entire people, otherwise it is but a jargon and not a language. Here (if we discount the slight confusion between a jargon and a separate private language) we have language considered as indissolubly related to an imaginary social and political organism. Tolomei and others also considered the prime purpose of language to be that of social intercourse.

In this respect, the Renaissance marks a definite step beyond the linguistic theories of antiquity and the Middle Ages. The general tendency to regard the Cinquecento as an age of pure individualism has led to the idea that language, also, was regarded in the Renaissance (as it has been in Scholastic philosophy) solely from the point of view of the individual. As a matter of fact, we must consider the Cinquecento as the time in which language first came to be regarded as a primarily social phenomenon.

C. LANGUAGE AS AN INDEPENDENT ORGANISM. Not only doctrines implying a 'social organism,' but also theories of language itself as an independent organism were present in some Cinquecento thinking. Varchi makes a comparison of the various stages of a language's existence with the four 'ages' of man; G. B. Gelli draws a detailed parallel between the development of a language and the condition of a human body in its different stages, and concludes by setting up for every language successive periods of 'growth', 'perfection', and 'decay', exactly comparable to those applied by Humboldt and Bopp to the development of the Indo-European tongues. Although it was mostly "Tuscans' who held such theories, the idea was widespread enough for Girolamo Ruscelli, an 'anti-Tuscan', also to make a comparison of language with a plant, and to draw a parallel with the grafting of pear and plum trees.

Others, of course, objected to this unjustified use of metaphor, and Peretto Pomponazzi, in Speroni's Dialogo, basing his arguments on the 'Aristotelian' theory that languages are created by man ad beneplacitum, declares that languages are not like trees or grasses, born into the world with different qualities and strengths, but that all derive their characteristics from the will of those who speak them. Trissino as well, in the person of the Castellano Rucellai, makes a sarcastic reference to his opponents' treatment of languages as having 'principio, vita e fine, come le febbri'.

2. Synchronic Aspects. Under this heading we shall treat briefly of the aspects of Renaissance theory which dealt with synchronic or descriptive analysis of language.

A. Criteria of Classification. In classifying or naming a language, one or more salient characteristics must be chosen in order to determine its relation to other languages. The Renaissance disputes between 'Tuscans' and 'anti-Tuscans', in so far as they touched upon criteria for linguistic classification, dealt mainly with the relative importance of phonetics versus vocabulary, and of the role of loan-words as determining elements.

The 'anti-Tuscans' based their concept of an Italian linguistic unity upon the presence of substantially the same vocabulary in a number of phonetically different, but mutually comprehensible dialects. Dante had already suggested that all of southern Europe was to be considered as sharing a single language, marked by the presence of many words in common, such as *Deus, caelum, mare,* and tripartite because of the use in different regions of three different affirmative particles: *oc, oïl,* and *sì.* The 'anti-Tuscans' of the Cinquecento, especially Trissino, in taking over Dante's theories, abandoned the obviously superficial criterium of the affirimative particle, but continued and developed his insistence upon the criterium of common vocabulary. It will be seen that such an insistence on vocabulary as the main determining characteristic of a language necessarily involves a relative neglect of phonetics and morphology.

The 'Tuscans', on the other hand, held to the smaller and more easily recognizable linguistic type of the local dialect, basing their views on the importance of phonetics and morphology as determining factors. Machiavelli, in his Dialogo, continually lays stress on 'modi, casi, differenze e accenti', as does Varchi in several places. The 'Tuscans', in fact, frequently went so far in their insistence on the phonetic differences as to make Tuscan seem more independent than it really was.

This distinction beween 'Tuscans' and 'anti-Tuscans' must not be exaggerated, however. Mme. Labande-Jeanroy has maintained that the 'anti-Tuscans' neglected phonetics and morphology completely as a criterium of differentiation. Such a thesis is hardly correct, in view of the fact that the 'anti-Tuscans' took into consideration and made frequent mention of phonetic and morphological factors. Trissino (who may be considered as best representing the 'anti-

Tuscans') speaks, in many passages of the Castellano, of 'pronunzie e modi di dire' in establishing linguistic divisions, and even goes so far as to declare that if French and Spanish had the same words and sounds, the same forms and syntax, as Italian, they would be one and the same language.

We must look somewhat deeper than a mere 'neglect of phonetics and morphology' for the root of the differences between the 'Tuscans' and the 'anti-Tuscans' on the point of vocabulary. The 'anti-Tuscans' as well as the 'Tuscans' recognized fully the actual existence of dialectal differences in Italy, and would hardly have denied the phonetic difference between, say, Florentine *famiglia* and Venetian *famegia*, or Flor. *pane* and Bolognese *pan*. But since the sounds in the various words showed a correspondence with each other, the 'anti-Tuscans' considered the phonetic differences as of less importance than the PHONEMIC correspondences, and were thus able to uphold lexical unity as a criterium of greater importance than purely phonetic similarity. The insistence of the 'Tuscans' on phonetics alone as a criterium, viewed in this light, appears decidedly restricted and narrow, in contrast with the broader phonemic viewpoint implicit in the doctrines of the 'anti-Tuscans'.

As a second criterium of classification, the presence of loan-words was considered by sixteenth-century critics to be of importance. To prove that the standard language, and especially Dante's usage in the Divine Comedy, was 'Italian' and not Tuscan or Florentine, the 'anti-Tuscans' pointed out the presence therein of words taken from other dialects. According to their doctrines, a language containing loan-words was no longer considered to be 'pure', but 'mixed'—or, in the case of Italian, 'italiano comune'. They did not admit intermediate possibilities; and they considered that, no matter how much the exterior phonological and morphological aspects of loan-words may have changed, they always remain foreigners, as it were, in the language which has adopted them.

The 'Tuscans' countered by maintaining that a language could not be considered as foreign to itself simply because of the presence of a few loan-words. Varchi goes even farther, and suggests that a majority of loan-words in the vocabulary would not 'denaturalize' a language. Machiavelli furnishes a sound scientific basis for this contention by pointing out that, when loan-words are taken into a language, they do not remain foreign in their sounds and grammatical features, but are adapted phonologically and morphologically to the system of the language adopting them. Here we have a clear statement of the nature of linguistic borrowing, and a striking anticipation of the phonemic doctrine, i.e. that every language moves in a specific series of characteristic speech-sounds or phonemes, to which loan-words are always adapted and whose later changes they follow.

B. GEOGRAPHICAL (DIALECTAL) DIVISIONS. The recognition of the multitude of Italian dialects dates from Dante, whose enumeration of the Italian dialects (De v. E. I.10) is valid even today. All writers of the Renaissance recognized the existence, not only of dialectal, but also of sub-dialectal and even municipal and individual differences, as pointed out above.

Cinquecento theorists were divided, however, in their attitude towards geographical classifications. Some anticipated the modern scientific attitude in wishing to recognize only objective and purely linguistic factors in classifying or naming dialects; others, however, held more closely to purely geographical and political—i.e. non-linguistic—considerations. This split was not along the line of 'Tuscan' versus 'anti-Tuscan', since we find both Trissino and Tolomei among the more objective theorists, and both Varchi and his opponent Muzio among the less objective scholars.

Trissino, for example, in his discussion of the 'Tuscan' arguments on behalf of a Florentine linguistic unity, has the Castellano reduce Filippo Strozzi's arguments to absurdity by pointing out the existence of sub-divisions within the Florentine dialect, and shows clearly the relativity of the nomenclature of the dialects, in contrast to the rigidity involved in upholding Florentine as the prime unity. This recognition of the relativity of dialectal classification, together with the perception of the individual as the fundamental linguistic unit, constitutes Trissino's best claim to merit as a linguist.

Tolomei, a 'Tuscan', recognized equally well the necessity of basing dialectal classifications not upon political provinces, but upon vocabulary, phonetics, and morphology, i.e. purely linguistic criteria. In upholding a broader Tuscan linguistic unity than that of Florence alone, he suggests the inclusion therein of not only sixteenth-century Tuscany, but of the equivalent of all ancient Etruria, because its inhabitants can learn Florentine more easily than others —i.e. because their tongue is in fact more similar to Florentine.

On the other hand, both 'Tuscans' and 'anti-Tuscans' are likewise represented in the number of those who preferred the more superficial limitation of dialectal classification to political division. Muzio, an 'anti-Tuscan', maintained that 'le lingue da individui non hanno da prendere il nome, ma dalle regioni dove si parlano', and that consequently, since the literary language was spoken and understood all throughout Italy, it should take its name from the whole region and be called Italian. But Varchi, whom Muzio was attacking, had also supported the same type of criterium for dialect divisions, saying 'le lingue si debbono chiamare dal nome di quei paesi, o vero luoghi, dove elle nascono'. The only difference between Varchi and Muzio lies in the extent of the geographical division that they chose to consider as the most important—the single town in Varchi's case, the country in Muzio's.

C. PHONETIC STUDY. Most of the disputes originated and were carried on mainly with reference to the written language and its use in literature; but rather more attention was given than has sometimes been supposed, to questions of the spoken language. At least one work, Varchi's Ercolano, was written with the definitely stated purpose of considering only spoken language, and several other men's work (that of Tolomei in the Cesano and the Polito, and Castelvetro in part of the Giunte and the Correzioni) was concerned chiefly with spoken usage. Not all the writers of the sixteenth century saw the necessity of distinguishing between the spoken and the written word, between the sound and the letter; but that this prime necessity of distinction was well recognized in some quarters, and for the first time, is obvious from the heated controversies in regard to orthographic reform, and from statements by Scaliger ('ab sonu est iudicandum, non ab litera') and by Varchi.

Investigations into phonetics and the nature of speech-sounds were carried out by several scholars, including Bartoli, J. C. Scaliger (who had an especial interest in the physiology of sound-production because of his profession as doctor) and Tolomei in the Polito.

D. MORPHOLOGICAL DISTINCTIONS. As is well known, the science of descriptive grammar was not far advanced in the sixteenth century; hence, most attempts at grammatical arrangement were made according to Greek and Latin models. Latin grammatical categories were transferred directly to Italian grammar, sometimes most inappropriately, as in Bembo's attempt to assign to the article the function of 'segnacaso' or case-sign. Others, however, such as Castelvetro in his Giunte and Tolomei in his 'trattatello' De' fonti de la lingua toscana, corrected such errors and contributed to the development of descriptive grammar based on the actual facts of the language.

The distinctions which were seen were, as might be expected mostly those between the ancient languages and modern Italian. The question of the 'regularity' of Italian received especial attention, and led to a clearer realization of the existence of grammatical order and categories in every language. The Latin humanists, in opposing the 'volgare', capitalized on that term to raise social prejudice because of its supposed connection with low-class persons, and also accused it of being an 'ungrammatical' language, i.e. not conforming to Latin grammatical criteria.

The defenders of the vernacular, in order to prove the difference of Italian grammar from that of Latin, and the equal worth of both, were thus obliged to investigate the nature of Italian. Even on the part of Latinists, the imperfections of the old concepts were seen by some, as in Scaliger's criticism of the old doctrines of the 'parts of speech', in his De Causis Linguae Latinae, on the grounds that it would not fit all cases, especially those in which one word is at the same time a whole sentence.

Tolomei goes even farther, passing beyond destructive criticism to a constructive affirmation in the Cesano of the existence of a natural grammatical regularity present in all languages, and of the speakers' normal adherence to the rules of their own language. Then, with a list of the phonetic, morphological, and syntactical differences between Latin and Italian, Tolomei proves conclusively the right of Italian to be considered a separate language with a grammar of its own.

Varchi, in one place in the Ercolano, makes yet a further step forward, with the suggestion, anticipating the conclusions of modern linguistics, that it is useless to speak of any language as being worth more or less than any other, since deficiencies in one respect (e.g. lack of passive and deponent verbs in Italian) are balanced by advantages in others (e.g. presence of articles and suffixes). Moreover, Varchi then goes on to establish a very important distinction, between outer grammatical form and inner meaning, showing a perception of the significance of grammatical form as a determinant of the character of a language, in the formal distinction between *sono amato, sei letto, è udito* in more than one word as opposed to *amor, legeris, auditur* in one word alone.

E. CORRECTNESS was an idea predominant in the Renaissance, as it is today, both as a heritage from ancient and mediaeval times, and in connection with aesthetic ideas of regularity and the imitation of models; and also in connection with intellectual or social standing. This idea was common to most 'Tuscans' and 'anti-Tuscans' alike. But the stand taken by Peretto Pomponazzi in Speroni's Dialogo is important is exemplifying a reaction against humanistic ideas or correctness or of necessary limitation of thought by linguistic form. Peretto vigorously asserts the equal values of all languages—Latin and Greek, Arabic and Hindu, Mantuan and Milanese—for philosophical discussion.

3. DIACHRONIC ASPECTS. In this section we shall consider the Renaissance theories on the historical development of language, the origin of Italian, and phonetic change.

A. LINGUISTIC CHANGE, as a principle, was inevitably suggested to the minds of Renaissance writers by the difference between Latin and Italian, and at the same time by the obvious relationship between them—a relationship too obvious to permit of fantasies ascribing to Italian a non-Latin origin, such as were thought up for French by Estienne and others in this same period. Dante was the first writer on language to evolve a theory of inevitable linguistic mutability, which he ascribed, in the manner of scholastic philosophy, to man's fundamental instability and variability in all his customs and manners. In the De vulgari Eloquentia we find the first version of Dante's theory, in which he considers Adam's language as having been exempted from this universal law of change, and as having been spoken unchanged down to the time of the erection of the tower of Babel. In Paradiso 26.124-126, however, he abandoned this exception too, and declared that even Adam's language had become completely extinct through change before the tower of Babel was begun. By the time of the Cinquecento, the fact of linguistic change was received without discussion (the principle having been ultimately accepted after the Bruni-Biondo debate), and argnment centered rather around its nature and causes.

B. THE ORIGIN OF ITALIAN was one of the first questions to arise. Dante, without indicating his belief as to the actual order of development of the Romance languages, had held that Latin had been established by a consensus of opinion to serve (as it did in his time) as an unchanging common language over and above the vernacular tongues. In the Cinquecento, however, it was generally recognized that Italian had developed out of Latin; the question was, how and under what impulses it had done so. Most scholars considered that the vernacular had resulted from a mixture of Latin with the language of the barbarian invaders, to a greater or less degree, and heated arguments (as in Muzio's attack on Varchi) occasionally arose as to exactly what tribes in what places had originated the new language.

As possible sources for both morphological and lexicological innovations in Italian, the tongues of the Germanic invaders were frequently cited, and also such less likely tongues as Hebrew (by Tolomei), Provençal (by Varchi), and Etruscan (by Muzio). An interesting passage is that in which Muzio, piqued by the accusations of impurity leveled against Italian by the humanists, turns their own weapons against them, and advances a theory of the origin of Latin from the combination of Etruscan with the language of the Latin invaders—whence he deduces that Latin is no more 'pure' than Italian.

In general, linguistic change was presumed to occur usually, and in any case much more rapidly, in the case of invasion and settlement of territory by new peoples, than as a result of gradual evolution of a language's 'inner form' of its own accord. This viewpoint we find elaborated by Machiavelli and by Tolomei; the former considers that, in the case of new settlement of a province, a language may change in a single lifetime.

C. PHONETIC CHANGE was by many Renaissance scholars presumed to occur in a haphazard way, with the 'throwing away' or 'insertion' of sounds quite at random. A great part of Renaissance linguistics was conducted on the same lines as ancient etymologizing, with very little conception of rigorous method: and, as in ancient etymologies of the 'lucus a non lucendo' type, more attention was paid to the explanation of a word's origin by comparison with words of similar appearance, even if of opposite meaning, than to investigation of the development of its phonetic elements. Bembo, for example, derived *madrigale* from *materiale* 'coarse, bastard (i.e. poetic form)', paying more attention to meaning than to phonetic development, thus putting the cart before the horse; Castelvetro ascribed *bue, lusignolo* to onomatopoetic origins. Ménage's derivation of *haricot* from *faba* belongs in this same class.

Varchi accepted this as the normal state of affairs; hence his well-known contempt for the fanciful and often ridiculous imaginings of the etymologists. This carried him too far, however, in the direction of exaggerating the 'ad placitum' theory in regard to phonetics, and of denying any possibility of explaining the development of words. The passage at the very end of Castelvetro's Correzione, where Castelvetro narrates his discussion with Varchi on the origin of the Itallian future tense, is very well known. In this passage, Castelvetro sets forth and proves from the examples, not only of *amerò*, but also of *leggerò* and *udirò*, the rule of the preservation intact of *-r-* from Latin to Italian, and of the origin of the composite future from the infinitive forms of *avere*.

Of even more importance than Castelvetro's intuition of regular sound-change, however, is the work of Claudio Tolomei, who many properly be hailed as the real forerunner of orderly, scientific examination of linguistic change. In t h e Cesano, treating of the development of *plenus, clavis,* and (*af*)*flatus* into *pieno, chiave,* and *fiato,* he suggests that in Old Tuscan all combinations of consonant plus *l* developed into consonant plus *i* (yod); and that words like *plora, implora, splende, plebe* and the like must therefore have been introduced in their original Latin form by writers. Otherwise, says Tolomei, we should have had **piora,* **impiora,* **spien-*

de, and *pieve*, which last we indeed have in the meaning 'country (i.e. plebeian) church'. In this passage Tolomei anticipates fully the chief contributions of nineteenth-century linguistic science. The hypothesis of regular sound-change; the distinction, which immediately follows therefrom between 'popular' and 'learned' words, and the recognition of pairs of 'doublets' with different meanings, representing different stages of the language; and the study of a word first from the phonetic point of view and then from the semantic, are all present in this passage from Tolomei, not only in embryo, but well developed. All that would have been necessary for the development of linguistic science two hundred and fifty years previous to its actual rise, would have been the careful application of Tolomei's method. Unfortunately, outside of Celso Cittadini (who took over Tolomei's ideas, but did not handle them exceptionally well), Tolomei had no successor, and hence one cannot call him the 'father', but only a very advanced precursor of modern linguistics.

In addition to Castelvetro and Tolomei, the Latinist Scaliger deserves mention as another in advance of his time with respect to scientific procedure; though, in his case, evidences of this are more fragmentary than in the case of other writers mentioned. Especially important are Scaliger's attempts at physiological explanations of sound-developments and other phenomena, and his use of what few data were available on ancient Latin forms to outline a few traits of historical grammar, as in his remark: *NATUS*, fuit enim *GNATUS*, a *GENEROR*. Unfortunately, Scaliger's information was often scanty or his intuitions as to the historical order of his data were at fault, so that his contribution remained quantitatively small, despite the improvement in method. The three above mentioned, however, mark a definite advance over the haphazard approach characteristic of the grammarians of the preceding epochs and of that century—an approach defended by Varchi as a necessary evil.

Why, however, did the occasional evidences of improvement in method, which we have tried to summarize in this chapter, remain only sporadic phenomena, and not spread to the whole field of language study, as they finally did in the nineteenth century? We can only suggest the probable influence of two currents prevalent in the seventeenth and eighteenth centuries, both of which were such in their nature as to discourage a scientific and historical approach. In the first place, the dogmatic, authoritarian, puristic attitude, which by the end of the sixteenth century was dominant in the field of belles-lettres and also among those who studied the Italian language most intensively (the 'Crusca' and their followers), was essentially unhistorical in its approach, setting up a fixed standard of value for all usage and for all periods, rather than attempting to determine the development and spread of the standard language. In the second place, the interest in 'general grammar' characteristic of the seventeenth and eighteenth centuries was conducive to seeking 'logical' categories (really, of course, the grammatical categories of Greek and Latin) in all linguistic manifestations, rather than to analysis of the phenomena themselves in their own right. It was not until these two attitudes were overcome in the nineteenth century that true scientific study of languages could be begun, in the Indo-European field by Rask and Grimm, and in the Romance field by Diez, Ascoli, and Meyer-Lübke.

Chapter V
The Significance of the Questione Della Lingua

What, then, is the significance of the Questione della Lingua, in its relation to the history of the Italian language itself? Were the theories propounded in the debates a positive influence, as some scholars (especially literary historians) have thought, or, on the other hand, as others have maintained, was the Questione della Lingua a subject of no importance whatsoever in the history of standard Italian? In this chapter, we intend to trace in parallel lines the development of theoretical discussion in relation to the spread of Florentine as the standard language, and in that way to arrive at a more definite conclusion concerning the relationship between the two. We shall discuss the situation prevailing in the four principal epochs treated in Chapter II: the time of Dante, the Renaissance, the seventeenth and eighteenth centuries, and the modern periods.

1. DANTE AND HIS TIME. Before the end of the thirteenth century, a relatively uniform standard language can scarely be said to have existed for the Italian peninsula. Various efforts have indeed been made, even recently, to prove that a 'volgare illustre' existed in Italy in periods anterior to the thirteenth century; but there is but slender evidence to support such a contention. In order to consider the various writings of Sicilians, Central Italians, Tuscans, and North Italians (even those with the highest literary aims) during the thirteenth century as manifestations of a single 'volgare aulico' or standard language, it is necessary to neglect linguistic criteria and so to water down the concept of 'standard' or 'unified' language as to render it useless.

The actual situation, linguistically, in the thirteenth century, was roughly as follows: non-literary material, when not written in Latin, was couched in the local dialect of the region of its origin. The same is true, to an only slightly lesser degree, of consciously literary works—e.g., the stylized Sicilian of the 'Scuola Siciliana', the Central Italian of the Ritmo Cassinese, the Lombard of Bonvesin da Riva, etc., as contrasted with the Tuscan of Dante and his contemporaries. Even Guittone d'Arezzo and thirteenth-century Sienese writers, for example, show marked dialectal peculiarities in contrast to Florentine. The problem facing any writer of Dante's time desiring to reach an audience not merely in his own town or province, but in all Italy, was that of finding a mode of speech understandable by all; which is the problem Dante attempts to solve in the first book of the De vulgari Eloquentia.

Now in appraising the solution of the 'volgare illustre', based on and common to all the Italian dialects, yet identical with none, as offered by Dante, we must be careful, at the same time that we recognize the advances in linguistic study which Dante made, nevertheless not to over-emphasize the scientific element in Dante's analysis. As has been pointed out repeatedly, Dante's use of his terms was not rigorous in the modern sense of scientific exactitude. More over, his main criterium in classifying linguistic divisions was that of the affirmative particle and of vocabulary: and with regard to phonetic differences, his main standard of judgment was that of aesthetic impression. In passing judgment on the various dialects, Dante bases his condemnatory decisions upon ethical and literary value-judgments.

Hence we must uphold the opinion which has, for the most part, prevailed in recent criticism, that the abstract type of language which Dante considered desirable as a standard for Italy was really nothing more than an abstraction, as yet unrealized in Dante's time, and the artificial formation and establishment of which was, as a matter of fact, contrary, not only to the normal course of events, but even to Dante's own usage. But the De vulgari Eloquentia is none the less important as a reflection of the problems facing the then nascent standard language, i.e. its formation, establishment, and use for literary purposes.

During the period following Dante's lifetime, the use of Florentine as a literary language was spread, despite the political disunity of Italy, by Tuscan activity and supremacy in two fields: literary and economic. The work of the great three—Dante, Petrarch and Boccaccio—and other Florentine writers had established a corpus of material imitation; and Tuscan, especially Florentine, manufacturing, commercial, and banking activity carried Tuscan speech and literature to the rest of Italy. (We must not over-emphasize the role of literature, or underestimate that of economic activity, in the spread of Tuscan; it would not be an exaggeration to say that 1252, the year when the first gold florin was coined, was a date of fully as great importance in the spread of Florentine speech as the date of any one work of literature.) In this period of gradual expansion among the aristocracy and bourgeoisie, the Italian standard language faced no new problems (any more than did the French or English languages in the same period); to this fact is due the quiescence of the Questione della Lingua in the period between Dante and the Cinquecento.

2. THE RENAISSANCE. During the fifteenth century, however, as is well known, the use of standard Italian in literature suffered a serious setback as a result of the absorption of most scholars' and men of letters' activities in the humanistic movement—a setback relatively more serious than that felt by French or English as a result of the same forces. There was a lag of nearly a century between the rise of humanism at the beginning of the Quattrocento and the re-assertion of the value of the vernacular towards the end of that century and the beginning of the Cinquecento. The explanation of this to be found in the relatively greater force of the humanistic movement in Italy, and the greater neglect into which the literary use of standard Italian fell as a result—cf. the well known failure of the Certame Coronario in 1441. Hence the debates on the standard language were also quiescent until such time as the new problems brought by its renewed use in literature arose at the beginning of the sixteenth century.

The great debates of the Cinquecento were concerned, for the most part, directly with the problems then confronting the use of the literary language, and the rest renewed questions that had already been settled in Dante's time and soon thereafter. Looked at from the point of view of the standard language, the four main problems needing solution were:

    a. The defense of the vernacular against humanistic Latin;

    b. The codification of Italian grammar, as an aid in its defense against Latin (and numberless questions of 'correctness' which arose as corollaries);

    c. The stage of the Italian language (archaic or modern) to be used as a model for literary usage; and

    d. Orthographical reform.

In addition to these, there were two apparent problems which really did exist, but which, being on a more superficial and hence more easily apprehended intellectual level, received even more discussion:

    e. The name to be applied to the standard language ('Florentine', 'Tuscan', or 'Italian'?); and

    f. The belated question which dialect (Tuscan or

some other) was actually or should be chosen for the literary language.

The close parallel between these problems and the subject-matter of the Questione della Lingua will be noted at once. The actual solutions which the problems received were as follows: Italian superseded Latin once again as the language of literature, humanism, and scholarship, and this solution was strengthened in the theoretical field by the discussions of such men as Bembo in his Prose della volgar Lingua. Codification of Italian grammar was accomplished through the work of Bembo, Fortunio, and others. The archaic or Trecento stage of Italian was established as the norm of usage in most branches of literary endeavor, primarily as a result of the influence of Bembo and his followers, but not without a great amount of opposition. In orthographical matters, some reforms were carried out, but not the more drastic changes proposed by Trissino.

The two illusory problems of the name of the standard language and the dialect to be chosen as literary language naturally failed to receive a definitive solution. It was an utterly irrelevant matter by what NAME the koiné was to be called, as the facts of the case were in no wise affected thereby. Those who opposed the use of Tuscan as literary language, or denied its Tuscan origin, simply failed to perceive that standard Italian had (and had had since the fourteenth century) a Florentine base. It is the futility of the arguments on these points—superficially the most prominent and most violently debated—that seems to have created an unfavorable impression of the Questione della Lingua in most critics' minds.

3. THE SEVENTEENTH AND EIGHTEENTH CENTURIES. In the course of the sixteenth century, the main lines were drawn along which the debates on the nature and use of

the standard language continued during the following centuries. In later times, Galvani repeats Varchi; Cesari repeats Bembo; Cesarotti and Perticari repeat Trissino. The situation at the time of Manzoni remained, so far as the theoretical arguments involved were concerned, exactly the same as it was at the time of Varchi.

What interests us more is the reason for this standstill of over two centuries' duration in the devolopment of the Questione della Lingua. Such a 'petrification', as it were, did not take place in France or England or Spain. In France, for example, after the problems discussed by Du Bellay in the Deffense et Illustration had been resolved (either positively or negatively) by the generation of Malherbe and Vaugelas, the question was at an end, and the debates lasted no longer. The answer is to be found, of course, in the situation of the standard language itself in Italy during those centuries.

The political disunity of Italy up to and through the Renaissance had not impeded the spread of standard Tuscan by economic and literary channels, and it may be fairly said that the sixteenth century had brought with it an essential (though not absolutely complete) linguistic unification of the upper classes. The differences between 'Italian' or 'lingua cortigiana' and 'Tuscan' speech, of which so much was made in the debates of the Questione della Lingua, were simply those between the generalized (and not wholly 'pure') Tuscan of the upper classes throughout Italy, on the one hand, and the strictly 'pure' and extremely idiomatic speech of Tuscany and Florence itself, on the other. The lower classes continued, of course, to speak in the local vernaculars, which were the object of contempt from 'Tuscans' and 'anti-Tuscans' alike.

Whereas in France, England, and Spain, however, the forces of political and economic unification extended the standard speech to the middle and lower classes during the seventeenth and following centuries, these forces were absent in seventeenth and eighteenth century Italy. The result was that, with Italy politically divided and under foreign rule or influence, and with the economic life of the country ruined, no extension of linguistic unification took place beyond the point it had reached in the sixteenth century—i.e. a situation where the standard speech was confined to the upper classes and the only unifying force left was the relatively weak influence of literature alone. As long as the standard language remained a purely upper-class and literary phenomenon, the problems confronting its further spread remained unsolved.

4. THE MODERN PERIOD. It was only when the post-Napoleonic era brought with it an effective desire for political unification, and eventual achievement of that aim, that the fundamental problem debated in the Questione della Lingua, the extension of a single standard language to all of Italy, was solved. In more recent years, linguistic unification has been further advanced by increased regional intercommunication, by schools, by the radio, by military training and other features of governmental centralization. That the solution has been essentially that favored by the 'Tuscan' and 'anti-archaistic' party—the so-called 'soluzione manzoniana'—has been repeatedly pointed out. It must also be remembered, though, that standard Italian, although based on Florentine, is not without dialectal elements as well, and the standard language is not so absolutely identical with Florentine as some puristic partisans of the 'Tuscan' doctrine have maintained.

In this connection, it is interesting to observe the change in the status of the dialects vis-à-vis the standard language in literary usage. As long as the standard language was not firmly established and its use was subject to doubt and debate, non-Tuscan writers of standard Italian were subject to psychological insecurity with regard to the value of their own local dialect, with the result that the latter came to be the object of contempt and was banished from use in elegant literary efforts. With the solution of the Questione della Lingua and the establishment of the standard language in the nineteenth century, this insecurity disappeared, and with it the hesitation concerning the use of dialect in literary works in standard Italian. This, together with the development of 'realistic' literary practice in the nineteenth century, is the explanation of the appearance of local dialects in the works of such writers as the North Italian Fogazzaro or the Sicilian Verga.

At present, the Questione della Lingua is a thing of the past, and of purely historical interest. The reason is not difficult to see: the problems facing the rise of the koiné have been solved, and hence the Questione della Lingua and its debates have become superfluous. It must be emphasized, however, that they were not superfluous (although frequently the debates were based on misunderstandings of the premises and were replete with irrelevancies) as long as the standard language itself faced the problems we have outlined. The debates of the Questione della Lingua in the Cinquecento and following centuries have the following significance, therefore: they were not a cause, but an effect, of the rise of the koiné, and were a faithful reflection of the problems facing standard Italian at the various critical points in its history.

Appendix I
Chronological Table of the Questione Della Lingua

In this table is given, for convenience of reference, a list in chronological order of the principal documents of the Questione della Lingua. More attention proportionately has been given to the Cinquecento than to later centuries, because of the greater importance of the Renaissance period; neither for the Cinquecento nor for later centuries, however, have documents of minor importance been listed. In some cases, the dates given are only approximative, inasmuch as exact dates are not available or are disputed. Where possible, the relation of works to each other has been indicated by cross-reference, and indication is given of the authors' stand on the questions of 'Tuscanism' and 'archaism'.

1. 1305 (ca.) Dante Alighieri: De vulgari Eloquentia. Anti-Tusc.
— 1435 Bruni-Biondo debate.
2. 1500-10 ca. Vincenzo Calmeta: Della lingua cortigiana (lost). Anti-Tusc., anti-arch.
3. 1500-15 ca. (pub. 1525) Pietro Bembo: Prose della volgar lingua. Tusc., arch. (Answer to §2.)
4. 1508 ff. (pub. 1528) Baldassar Castiglione: Il Cortegiano. Anti-Tusc., anti-arch. (Propounds doctrines of §2.)
5. 1509-11 (It. vers.; def. ed. 1525) Mario Equicola: Della natura di Amore. Anti-Tusc.
6. 1514 ca. Niccolò Machiavelli: Dialogo intorno alla nostra lingua. Tusc. (Answer to §1.)
7. 1524 Gian Giorgio Trissino: Lettera a Papa Clemente premessa alla Sofonisba. Anti-Tusc., anti-arch. Orthographical reform.
8. 1524-5 Agnolo Firenzuola: Discacciamento delle nuove lettere inutilmente aggiunte nella lingua toscana. (Answer to §7.)
9. 1524-5 Lodovico Martelli: Risposta alla epistola del Trissino. Tusc. (Answer to §7.)

10.	1524-5	Adriano Franci (Claudio Tolomei): De le lettere nuovamente aggiunte, libro intitolato Il Polito. Tusc. (Answer to §7.)
11.	1524-5	Niccolò Liburnio (C. Tolomei: Dialogo sopra la lettera del Trissino. (Answer to §7.)
12.	1529	Romolo Amaseo: Orazione contro il volgare.
13.	1529	G. G. Trissino: Translation of De vulgari Eloquentia.
14.	1529	G. G. Trissino: Il Castellano. Anti-Tusc., anti-arch. (Defense of §§7, 13.)
15.	1530 ca.	Sperone Speroni: Dialogo della lingua. Partly anti-Tusc., anti-arch.; partly Tusc., arch.
16.	1530-6	Girolamo Muzio: Battaglie in difesa dell' italica lingua. Anti-Tusc., anti-arch.
17.	1535 ca. (pub. 1554-5)	C Tolomei: Il Cesano. Tusc., anti-arch.
18.	1546	Giovanni Battista Gelli: Capricci del Bottaio. Tusc., anti-arch.
19.	1546	Pier Francesco Giambullari: Il Gello. Tusc., anti-arch.
20.	1550	Lodovico Dolce: Osservazioni nella volgar lingua. Tusc.
21.	1551	G. B. Gelli: Discorso sopra la difficoltà di ordinare la lingua di Firenze. Tusc., anti-arch.
22.	1553	Girolamo Ruscelli: Lettera a M. Lodovico Dolce. Anti-Tusc.
23.	1550's	Lodovico Castelvetro: Giunte alle prose del Bembo. Anti-Tusc., anti-arch. (Criticisms of §3.)
24.	bef. 1565 (pub. 1570)	Benedetto Varchi: L'Ercolano. Tusc., anti-arch.
25.	1572	L. Castelvetro: Correzione di alcune cose nel dialogo delle lingue di M. B. Varchi. Anti-Tusc., anti-arch. (Answer to §24.)
26.	1573 (pub. 1582)	G. Muzio: La Varchina. Anti-Tusc., arch. (Answer to §24.)
27.	1584-6	Leonardo Salviati: Gli avvertimenti della lingua sopra il Decamerone. Tusc., arch.
28.	1585	L. Salviati: Stacciate contro la Gerusalemme Liberata. Tusc., arch.
29.	1595-1601	Celso Cittadini: Trattato della vera origine e del progresso e nome della nostra lingua. Tusc.
30.	1600	C. Cittadini: Sulla formazione della lingua toscana.
31.	1604	C. Cittadini: Dell' origine della toscana favella.

32.	1612	Vocabolario dell' Accademia della Crusca. Tusc., arch.
33.	1612	Paolo Beni: Anticrusca. Anti-Tusc., anti-arch. (Attack on §32.)
34.	1612	Alessandro Tassoni: Pensieri diversi. Anti-Tusc., anti-arch.
35.	1613-14	Orlando Pescetti and Benedetto Fioretti: Polemic replies to §33.
36.	1614	Michelangelo Fonte (P. Beni): Il Cavalcante. (Reply to §35; further attack on §32.)
37.	1616	P. Beni: Commento sulla Gerusalemme Liberata. Anti-Tusc., anti-arch. (Reply to §§28, 32, 35.)
38.	1617	Adriano Politi: Sulla vera denominazione della lingua volgare. Tusc.
39.	1626	Ferdinando di Diano: Fiume dell' origine della lingua italiana e latina.
40.	1652	Ovidio Montalbani: Dialogia, ovvero delle cagioni e della naturalezza del parlare, e specialmente del più antico e più puro bolognese. Anti-Tusc.
41.	1653	O. Montalbani: Cronoprostasi Falsinea, ovvero le Saturnali Vindicie del parlare bolognese e lombardo.
42.	1655-68	Daniello Bartoli: Il torto e il diritto del non si può. Tusc., anti-arch.
43.	1657	Carlo Dati: Dell' obbligo di ben parlare la propria lingua. Tusc., arch.
44.	1685	Egidio Ménage: Le origini della lingua italiana.
45.	1690	Gian Vincenzo Gravina: Sull' uso della lingua italiana, dialogo latino. Tusc., arch.
46.	1694	Cristoforo Cellario: De origine linguae italicae.
47.	1695	Anton Maria Salvini: Discorsi accademici. Tusc., arch.
48.	1706	Girolamo Gigli: Orazione in lode della toscana favella.
49.	1707	G. Gigli: Dizionario cateriniano. Tusc. but anti-Flor.
50.	1708	G. V. Gravina: Ragion poetica. Tusc., arch.
51.	1715	A. M. Salvini: Prose toscane. Tusc., arch.
52.	1717	Niccolò Amenta: Osservazioni al libro del Bartoli 'Il torto e il diritto del non si può'. Tusc., arch.
53.	1717 (pub. 1723)	N. Amenta: Della lingua nobile d'Italia. Tusc., arch.

54.	1731	A. M. Biscioni: Note al Malmantile. Tusc., arch.
55.	1732-5 (pub. 1737)	Giulio Cesare Becelli: Se oggidì, scrivendo, si debba usare la lingua italiana del buon secolo. Tusc., arch. (ultra-puristic).
56.	1737	Domenico Maria Manni: Lezioni di lingua toscana. Tusc., arch.
57.	1739	Francesco Arizzi: Il toscanismo e la Crusca, tragicommedia giocosa. Anti-Tusc.
58.	1740	Carlo Donadoni: La Crusca in esame. Anti-Tusc.
59.	1740	Gregorio Bessani: Discorso intorno alla lingua italiana. Tusc., arch.
60.	1740	Paolo Gagliardi: Cento osservazioni di lingua. Tusc., arch.
61.	1759	Onofrio Branda: Della lingua toscana. Tusc., arch.
62.	1760	Giuseppe Parini: Al padre On. Branda milanese. Not anti-Tusc., but defends dialects.
63.	1765	Giuseppe Baretti: Diceria d'Aristarco Scannabue (Frusta lett. no. 25.) Anti-Tusc., anti-arch.
64.	1771	Uberto Benvoglienti: Opuscoli diversi. (Including: Dialogo sopra la volgar lingua; Osservazioni sull' origine, progresso e cambiamenti della lingua toscana; Storia della lingua italiana.) Tusc.
65.	1777	Girolamo Rosasco: Della lingua toscana dialoghi 7. Tusc., arch.
66.	1785	Melchiorre Cesarotti: Saggio sulla filosofia delle lingue. Anti-Tusc., anti-arch., Gall.
67.	1789	G. B. de Velo: Sulla preeminenza di alcune lingue e sull'autorità degli scrittori approvati e dei grammatici. Tusc., arch., anti-Gall. (Answer to §66.)
68.	1791	Gian Francesco Galeani Napione: Dell' uso e dei pregi della lingua italiana libri III. Anti-Gall. (Answer to §66.)
69.	1810	Antonio Cesari: Dissertazione sopra lo stato presente della lingua italiana.
70.	1813	A. Cesari. Le Grazie, dialogo. Tusc., arch.
71.	1813	Lorenzo Pignotti: Storia della Toscana. Tusc. (Answer to §66.)
72.	1817-26	Vincenzo Monti: Proposta di alcune correzioni ed aggiunte al Vocabolario della Crusca. Anti-Tusc.

73.	1818	Giulio Perticari: Degli scrittori del Trecento e de' loro imitatori. Anti-Tusc., anti-arch.
74.	1820	G. Perticari: Dell' amor patrio di Dante e del suo libro intorno il Volgare Eloquio. Anti-Tusc., anti-arch.
75.	1820	Giuseppe Luigi Biamonti: Lettere di Panfilo a Polifilo sopra l'apologia del libro Della Volgare Eloquenza di Dante. Tusc. (Answer to §74.)
76.	1825	Niccolò Tommaseo: Il Perticari confutato da Dante. Tusc., arch. (Answer to §74.)
77.	1826	Alessandro Manzoni: Lettera al padre Cesari Tusc., anti-arch.
78.	1830	Giovanni Galvani: Della lingua. Tusc.
79.	1833	Basilio Puoti: Della maniera di studiare la lingua. Tusc., anti--arch.
80.	1834	G. Galvani. Sulla verità delle dottrine perticariane nel fatto storico della lingua, dubbi. Tusc. (Answer to §§73, 74.)
81.	1845	A. Manzoni: Lettera a Giacinto Carena sulla lingua italiana. Tusc., anti-arch.
82.	1868	A. Manzoni: Dell' unità della lingua e dei mezzi di diffonderla, relazione. Tusc., anti-arch.
83.	1872	Graziadio Isaia Ascoli: Proemio all' Archivio Glottologico Italiano. Anti-Tusc.
84.	1927	Vasco Restori: Contro corrente. Belated Anti-Tusc.
85.	1939	Bruno Migliorini: Lingua contemporanea. Questione della Lingua treated as finished.

Appendix II
Notes and Citations

In this section, a brief general bibliography will be given, and then notes on passages in the text of the first five chapters. For more detailed bibliography, reference may be made to the author's Bibliography of Italian Linguistics 426-431, and to the material contained in Vivaldi, Belardinelli, and Labande-Jeanroy.

1. GENERAL BIBLIOGRAPHY (in chronological order of publication).

Luzzatto, Leone: Pro e contro Firenze. Saggio storico sulla polemica della lingua. Verona-Padova, 1893; pp. 111.

Vivaldi, Vincenzo: Le controversie intorno alla nostra lingua dal 1500 ai giorni nostri. Catanzaro, 1894-1898; 3 vols.

Belardinelli, Giuseppe: La questione della lingua; vol. I, Da Dante a Girolamo Muzio. Roma, 1904; pp. xv, 288.

Lanbande-Jeanroy, Thérèse: La question de la langue en Italie. Strasbourg, 1925; pp. 264.

Labande-Jeanroy, T.: La question de la langue en Italie de Baretti à Manzoni. Paris, 1925; pp. xiv, 133.

Vivaldi, V.: Storia delle controversie linguistiche in Italia da Dante ai nostri giorni. I. (Da Dante a M. Cesarotti). Catanzaro, 1925; pp. 245.

2. NOTES ON INDIVIDUAL PASSAGES. In this section will be included primarily citations of the original of important passages summarized in the text. References to the text will be by chapter and section number.

I.1.: On the opposition to Italian during the Renaissance, cf. V. Cian, Contro il volgare, Studi letterari e linguistici dedicati a Pio Rajna 251-297 (1911).

1.2.c: On the problem of Gallicism in the eighteenth

century, cf. A. Schiaffini, Aspetti della crisi linguistica italiana del Settecento, ZRPh. 57.275-295 (1937).

I.3.: On orthographical reform in Italian and its history, cf. F. Zambaldi, Delle teorie ortografiche in Italia, AIVeneto 50.323-368 (1892); G. Hartmann, Zur Geschichte der italienischen Orthographie, RF 20.199-283 (1907). For Tolomei's role, cf. F. Sensi, M. Claudio Tolomei e le controversie sull' ortografia italiana nel secolo XVI, RALincei IV.6.314-325 (1889).

II.1: For Dante's De vulgari Eloquentia and his philosophy of language, cf. F. d'Ovidio, Sul trattato De vulgari Eloquentia di Dante Alighieri, AGl. 2.59-110 (1876), and the same writer's Dante e la filosofia del linguaggio, AANapoli 25.1.271-303 (1892).

On the Bruni-Biondo debate and the question of plebeian Latin, cf. G. Mignini, La epistola di Flavio Biondo 'De locutione romana', Propugnatore NS.3.1.135-161 (1890); U. T. Holmes, Jr., The Vulgar Latin question and the origin of the Romance tongues, StP 25.51-61 (1928); F. Strauss, Vulgärlatein und Vulgärsprache im Zusammenhang d e r Sprachenfrage im 16. Jahrhundert (Frankreich und Italien), Marburg, 1938, pp. 131.

IV: On Renaissance grammar in general, cf. C. Trabalza, Storia della grammatica italiana, Milano, 1908, pp. xiv, 561; L. Kukenheim, Contributions à l'histoire de la grammaire italienne, espagnole et française à l'époque de la Renaissance, Amsterdam, 1932, pp. 232.

IV.1.a: Trissino's recognition of individual differences in speech:

... perocchè ciascun uomo, e casa e contrada, ha qualche particulare proprietà di parlare, che l'altro non ha; verbigrazia, Palla mio fratello ha qualche particulare proprietà del suo parlare, che non l'ho io; e Lorenzo vostro fratello n'ha qualcuna che non l'avete voi, e così parimente la nostra casa ha qualche differenza di parlare dalla vostra, e la nostra contrada da un' altra, e simili. (Castellano 32, ed. Milan, 1864.)

Varchi's recognition of individual differences:

E ardirei di dire che non pure tutte le città hanno diversa pronuncia l'una dall' altra, ma ancora tutte le castella; anzi chi volesse sottilmente considerare, come tutti gli uomini hanno nello scrivere differente mano l'uno dall' altro, così hanno ancora differente pronunzia nel favellare; onde non so come si possa salvare il Trissino, quando dice nel principio della sua Epistola a Papa Clemente: *Considerando io la pronunzia Italiana.* (L'Ercolano, Quesito Primo.)

IV.1.b: Varchi's connection of language with an entire people:

Varchi. Lingua, ovvero linguaggio, non è altro che un favellare d'uno o più popoli, il quale o i quali usano, nello sprimere i loro concetti, i medesimi vocaboli nelle medesime significazioni e co' medesimi accidenti.

Conte Ercolani. Perchè dite voi *d'un popolo?*

Varchi. Perchè, se parecchi amici o una compagnia, quantunque grande, ordinassero un modo di favellare tra loro, il quale non fosse inteso, nè usato se non da sè medesimi, questo non si chiamerebbe lingua, ma gergo, o in alcuno altro modo, come le cifere non sono propriamente scritture, ma scritture in cifere. (L'Ercolano, Quesito Primo.)

IV.1.c: Peretto's objections to animistic theories of language, in Speroni's Dialogo:

. . . io non vorrei che voi ne parlaste come di cose dalla natura prodotta, essendo fatte, e regolate dallo artificio delle persone a beneplacito loro, non piantate, nè seminate . . . Dunque non nascono le lingue per sè medesime, a guisa d'alberi, o d'erbe, quale debbole et inferma nella sua spezie, quale robusta et atta meglio a portar la somma di nostri umani concetti; ma ogni loro vertù nasce al mondo dal voler de' mortali.

IV.2.a: Trissino's criterium of a common vocabulary:

. . . nè mi può ancora cadere nell' anima, che i vocaboli che sono a tutte lingue d'Italia comuni, com'è *Dio, amore, cielo,* eccetera, et altri quasi infiniti, debbiano più tosto chiamarsi della lingua toscana, che dell' altre che parimenti gli hanno; i quali senza dubbio di niuna lingua d'Italia sono propri, ma sono comuni di tutte.

Machiavelli on loan-words and their adaptation in the borrowing language:

Aggiugnesi a questo che, qualunque volta viene o nuove dottrine in una città o nuove arti, è necessario che vi venghino nuovi vocaboli, e nati in quella lingua donde quelle dottrine e quelle arti son venute; ma riducendosi, nel parlare, con i modi, con i casi, con le differenze e con gli accenti, fanno una medesima consonanza con i vocaboli di quella lingua che trovano, e così diventano suoi; perchè, altrimenti, le lingue parrebbono rappezzate e non tornerebbono bene. E così i vocaboli forestieri si convertono in fiorentini, non i fiorentini in forestieri; nè però diventa altro la nostra lingua che fiorentina.

IV.2.d: Tolomei's affirmation of the existence of natural grammatical regularity in all languages:

Ch'ella [la Toscana lingua] sia vagabonda, e senza regole discorrere, chi crederà mai, quando che ogni lingua abbia la grammatica sua, senza la quale nè parlare nè lingua dir si potrebbe, nè già credo io che in questa dicesse alcun, *io amò, tu amo*. Benchè può esser che le regole che vi sono, non siano ancora o trovate o scritte, come in tutte sempre è avvenuto; conciossiacosachè la grammatica nasce dalla lingua, e non la lingua dalla grammatica. (Il Cesano 65, ed. Milan, 1864.)

IV.2.e: Peretto, in Speroni's Dialogo, on the equal value of all languages:

Io ho per fermo, che le lingue d'ogni paese, così l'Arabica e l'Indiana, come la Romana e l'Ateniese, siano d'un medesimo valore, et da mortali ad un fine con un giudizio formate ... le quali usiamo sì come testimoni del nostro animo, significando tra noi i concetti dell' intelletto.

To the humanist Lascaris' contention that 'diverse lingue sono atte a significare diversi concetti, alcune i concetti di dotti, alcune altre degli indotti', Peretto replies:

Più tosto vo' credere ad Aristotile, et alla verità, che lingua alcune del mondo (sia qual si voglia) non possa aver da sè stessa privilegio di significare i concetti del nostro animo; ma tutto consista nello arbitrio delle persone, onde chi vorrà parlar di filosofia con parole Mantovane o Milanesi, non gli può esser disdetto a ragione, più che disdetto gli sia il filosofare, et l'intender la cagion delle cose.

IV.3.a: Dante wrote in the De vulgari Eloquentia concerning the inevitability of linguistic change:

Cum igitur omnis nostra loquela, praeter illam homini primo concreatam a Deo, sit a nostro beneplacito reparata post confusionem illam, quae nil fuit aliud quam prioris oblivio, et homo sit instabilissimum atque variabilissimum animal, nec durabilis nec continua esse potest; sed sicut alia quae nostra sunt, puta mores et habitus, per locorum temporumque distantias variari oportet.

In Paradiso 26.124-132, Dante extends this theory to all human speech, even that of Adam and his descendants:

La lingua ch'io parlai fu tutta spenta
innanzi ch'all'ovra inconsummabile
fosse la gente di Nembròt attenta;
Chè nullo effetto mai razionabile
per lo piacere uman che rinovella
seguendo il cielo, sempre fu durabile.
Opera naturale è ch'uom favella,
ma così o così, natura lascia
poi fare a voi, secondo che v'abbella.

IV.3.c: Tolomei on regularity of phonetic development:

... e ardirei dire che nel primo e puro parlar degli uomini toscani questa fosse universale e verissima regola, e tutti quei vocaboli, che ora altrimenti s'usano e scritti si trovano, come *plora, implora, splende, plebe* e simili, non fussero presi dal mezzo delle piazze di Toscana; ma poste innanzi dagli scrittori, e da qualche ingegno, che volse la lingua arricchire, che gli parse usargli, come nelle stampe latine gli trovò, senza dar loro forma di toscan parlare . . . perchè senza dubbio il comune uso di quel secolo averebbe, se egli avesse quei vocaboli ricevuto, *piora, impiora, spiende* e *pieve* detto, come di questo ultimo ne abbiamo manifesto segno, che volgarmente Pieve si chiama quella sorte di chiesa ordinata alla religione di una plebe. (Cesano 66, 67.)

V.1.: We may mention the most recent effort to revive the theory that the 'volgare aulico' really existed: A. Ewert, Dante's theory of language, MLR 35.355-366 (1940).

The Department of Romance Studies Digital Arts and Collaboration Lab at the University of North Carolina at Chapel Hill is proud to support the digitization of the North Carolina Studies in the Romance Languages and Literatures series.

www.ingramcontent.com/pod-product-compliance
Lightning Source LLC
Chambersburg PA
CBHW020422230426
43663CB00007BA/1276